PENGUIN BOOKS

THE LIFTING DRESS

LAUREN BERRY received a BA from Florida State University and an MFA from the University of Houston, where she won the Inprint Paul Verlaine Prize in Poetry and served as poetry editor for *Gulf Coast*. In 2009–2010, she held the Diane Middlebrook Fellowship at the University of Wisconsin. She lives in Houston.

D1167219

THE NATIONAL POETRY SERIES

The National Poetry Series was established in 1978 to ensure the publication of five poetry books annually through five participating publishers. Publication is funded by the Lannan Foundation, Stephen Graham, Joyce & Seward Johnson Foundation, Glenn and Renee Schaeffer, Juliet Lea Hillman Simonds, and the Edward T. Cone Foundation.

2010 COMPETITION WINNERS

LAUREN BERRY OF HOUSTON, TEXAS, *The Lifting Dress*
Selected by Terrance Hayes, to be published by Penguin Books

WILLIAM BILLITER OF CLINTON, NEW YORK, *Stutter*
Selected by Hilda Raz, to be published by University of Georgia Press

JAMES GRINWIS OF FLORENCE, MASSACHUSETTS, *Exhibit of Forking Paths*
Selected by Eleni Sikelianos, to be published by Coffee House Press

M.A. VIZSOLYI OF NEW YORK, NEW YORK, *The Lamp with Wings:
Love Sonnets*
Selected by Ilya Kaminsky, to be published by HarperCollins Publishers

LAURA WETHERINGTON OF ROANOKE, VIRGINIA, *A Map Predetermined
and Chance*
Selected by C.S. Giscombe, to be published by Fence Books

the LIFTING DRESS

LAUREN BERRY

PENGUIN BOOKS

PENGUIN BOOKS

Published by the Penguin Group

Penguin Group (USA) Inc., 375 Hudson Street, New York, New York 10014, U.S.A.

Penguin Group (Canada), 90 Eglinton Avenue East, Suite 700, Toronto,

Ontario, Canada M4P 2Y3 (a division of Pearson Penguin Canada Inc.)

Penguin Books Ltd, 80 Strand, London WC2R 0RL, England

Penguin Ireland, 25 St Stephen's Green, Dublin 2, Ireland (a division of Penguin Books Ltd)

Penguin Group (Australia), 250 Camberwell Road, Camberwell,

Victoria 3124, Australia (a division of Pearson Australia Group Pty Ltd)

Penguin Books India Pvt Ltd, 11 Community Centre, Panchsheel Park, New Delhi - 110 017, India

Penguin Group (NZ), 67 Apollo Drive, Rosedale, Auckland 0632,

New Zealand (a division of Pearson New Zealand Ltd)

Penguin Books (South Africa) (Pty) Ltd, 24 Sturdee Avenue,

Rosebank, Johannesburg 2196, South Africa

Penguin Books Ltd, Registered Offices:

80 Strand, London WC2R 0RL, England

First published in Penguin Books 2011

10 9 8 7 6 5 4 3 2 1

Page vii constitutes an extension of this copyright page.

Library of Congress Cataloging in Publication Data

Berry, Lauren.

The lifting dress / Lauren Berry.

p.   cm.

ISBN 978-0-14-311965-4

I. Title.

PS3602.E76378L54   2011

811'.6—dc22   2011006502

Printed in the United States of America

Set in Goudy Oldstyle Std

Designed by Ginger Legato

To Edith LeBas

ACKNOWLEDGMENTS

Grateful acknowledgments to the editors of the following magazines, which first published the following poems, often in younger versions.

"The Pale-Skinned Catholic Girls Go Topless Sunbathing" *American Literary Review* (forthcoming)

"The Sawgrass Women Make Me Nervous" *Hayden's Ferry Review*; *Cream City Review*

"In the Bitter Orange Theater, a Child Who Has Never Seen Snow" (formerly titled "On the Stage of the Bitter Theater, a Child Who Has Never Seen Snow") *Hayden's Ferry Review*

"Be a Good Girl, Don't Tell" *Whiskey Island*

"The Just-Bled Girl Refuses to Speak" *Cream City Review*

"Seventh Grade Science in the Partially Burned Classroom" *Iron Horse Literary Review*

"Invitation from My Father to Observe Surgery" *Iron Horse Literary Review*

"Song for the Only Other Woman in the Slaughterhouse" *Verse Wisconsin*

"Notes on How My Mother Gets into Bed" *Verse Wisconsin*

"The Year My Mother and I Mistook the Pool for a Father" *Verse Wisconsin*

"Notes on How to Love a Boy" *Denver Quarterly*

"On Sunday Nights I Paint the Big Man's Wife" *Denver Quarterly*

I would like to thank Inprint, whose passionate support of writers helped make this book possible.

Thanks to my editor, Paul Slovak, for understanding my vision for this collection and supporting me through its development. Your guidance has been invaluable.

To Quan Barry, Amaud Jamaul Johnson, Jesse Lee Kercheval, Ron Kuka, Judy Mitchell, and Ron Wallace at the Wisconsin Institute for Creative Writing. The gift of the Diane Middlebrook Poetry Fellowship allowed this book to grow into adulthood.

To my mentors Mark Doty, J. Kastely, Tony Hoagland, Nick Flynn, Barbara Hamby, Erin Belieu, and David Kirby. Thank you for your rigor, your generosity, and your patience.

To the friends who teach me what it means to be a poet: Allison Eir Jenks, Kent Shaw, Glenn Shaheen, Hayan Charara, Craig Beaven, Nancy Reddy, and Erinn Batykefer.

To Tray Shellberg, for his unwavering love and belief in my art.

And to my family, who did not doubt me.

Contents

I am mad the way all young girls are mad,
with an offering, an offering . . .

—Anne Sexton, *Love Poems*

the
LIFTING DRESS

The entire red carnation in my mouth.

Like any panicked schoolgirl, I'm inarticulate
and constantly introduced

to beautiful things. Today it's a doctor
who says, *Young La-dy!* and demands,

Young La-dy, you cannot keep that garden

in your throat. How will we ask you questions?
How will you sip from the glass of water

and tell us what he did to you? Softly, I slip

the red carnation further into my throat.
There must be hundreds

of ways to be a girl. I'm just the kind
who has trouble parting her lips.

My mother left handwritten notes
on her sweet gum trees to warn boys
who cut through our backyard.

Wasp Nets. Do Not Enter.
With Scotch tape and spelling error, my mother
told the bad boys of the neighborhood not

to come near me. This was after I,
indolent in a rusted lawn chair, did nothing

when a blond boy flailed, screamed,
swelled down the steps of our pool
with lady-wasps swarming his arms.

Mother's phone calls were followed
by the red yawns of ambulance lights,
followed by the air-conditioned waiting
and the hospital bills she now owed the boy's father.

Mother cried over her practiced signature,
struggled to understand her handwriting, the fine
print. Those next few days I did not dare

the backyard, but every chance I got I flitted
into the pool and hid myself
under water. Under wasp wings.

I wanted stingers instead of leg hair.
Instead of legs. I put my mouth to the screen door
and listened for hives. The wasp world

was one that loved boys
as wrong as I did. Why was it that our mission
was to make men less beautiful?

Red. Wrecked. Those insects rushed to his eyelids
without fear. Of all the women
in the world, I find my sisters here.

THE PALE-SKINNED CATHOLIC GIRLS GO TOPLESS SUNBATHING

We could divide,
so easily,
our body parts

by color. At night
we lined up

in the alley behind
the town drugstore
and poured bottles

of whole milk
over our shoulders.

We eased
our hairless bodies

while the mothers
of younger girls

gasped from behind
balcony drapes. They
tossed down

ten-dollar rosaries.
To be sunburned was

an act of God, the triangles
glowing through the blow

of our white skirts.
We believed the world

was with us. How else
would a man know

which parts he could not touch?

SEVENTH GRADE SCIENCE IN THE PARTIALLY BURNED CLASSROOM

The way Sister Mary Dion told us about the calorie made it seem
    like something I could believe in. *The calorie*, she said,

as though it were a red wolf in a forest,

    the calorie, she said with wrinkled, gypsied hands,
is a unit of heat. It can raise one gram of water

    one degree. Heat. I whispered, *I knew it.*

I knew there were red wolves in my body, knew
    what went past my lips was adding to me.

In the middle of the night, I'd wake in sweat

    with a little more breast, already shifting
from the thin virgin in my skirt. I could leave her

    in my skirt if I burned it. I was in love with this idea;

every morning I brought a mirror to the table and left
    my jaw open so wide—*In wolf, in wolf, in wolf.*

But usually we walk the swamp in silence,

one behind the other. Me, wishing
my body looks good as hers

from behind. Today in the red mangrove
there's a dead dog. Stiff. There's a bolt

of white cotton around the dog. Which looks
like the dog is wearing a T-shirt.
Like the dog is a child with outstretched arms.

The Big Man's body tasted
like the apartment my father rented
when I was in the third grade.

It reminded me
of my father's girlfriend,
how she counted her ribs
in the reflection of my dollhouse.

Her dress raised
until my teacups uncracked
with the scent of wilt. Rot.

When the Big Man held my body,
I pictured my father
hunched over the apartment's wet bar
with his bottle of Windex.

He polished the glasses that read,
Name Your Poison.
As a girl, I didn't understand
that command. I didn't know

how soon I would lift
my head from a man's ink-stained hips
and attempt to tell him,
It tastes like poison.

Instead I wiped my tongue with
a page from the phone book. Words
in my mouth for the first time.

The telephone numbers of strangers
who knew how to say *your* and *poison*
and *tastes*. Words are the poison I name.

Leaning in a desk chair, the Big Man
plucked a dead wasp from the drapes
and tilted it into my water glass

but I took off, rambled
to the oval bathroom mirror

where I watched a girl
wake inside me
with a throat like a hallway
where rich folks are introduced.

It was then I knew
what my father mixed
in all those glasses

while his girlfriend put her tongue
to our family photograph

and I sat in his closet, humming
that song about the blind horses
and I cleaned the makeup from his shoes.

Big Sister Drinks in the Field Behind the Children's Hospital

I should never have been allowed
to be more than a child.

In my sister's mouth,
a flow of peach syrup.
I let it flood. I pulled her
from the Oldsmobile to give her air

though she fell back on top of me
and the schnapps bottle fell, never
breaking. It rolled from her mouth

while, across the field,
men cut out children's hearts.

My older sister.
I was not letting go.

Under my sister's body,
my blood flooded
with possibility:

If one of us stopped breathing,
I wanted it to be me. I
would not let her leave.

Is it true, my heart could be
the wet peach that sugars

her lips? Or could I be the baby
in the jar that has held other babies?

At fourteen I thought
it was the perfect way to die:
my sister above me and the field below,

dry as a dream and the seeds,
they blew through my hair. I believed

I was her temporary god,

though in the morning, when we woke
in our clothes, she said she lived
because she never

mistook the lighted rooms
of the hospital
for Heaven. I said,

If there is a Heaven,
I'm not letting you go.

In the Bitter Orange Theater, a Child Who Has Never Seen Snow

Paper snow on my swan costume, I try not
to prick the other girls

with the unhinged safety pin
in my palm. Surrounded

by this desperate season,
the fury of silver sequin,
the same shade

as the walls of my mother's
preordered coffin, I am told

to dance over a frozen lake.
I pirouette until the sweat . . .

It is not winter. There is no winter.

In this town, seasons change
when a stage mother
holds out a rolled-down silver leotard

and places my hand on her shoulder—
Step into it. Right leg. Left leg.

And then it's winter.

When the recital ends, the heavy velvet
swaying serious, she rolls my costume

down and returns my hand
to her other-mother shoulder. White

paper octagons jigsaw
to the dressing room floor.
Does my body have its own winter?

I shouldn't be sweating like this—
but how else

do I let her know, this woman
who can never be mine,

that this *is* a season
in which a mother can hunt?

Discover me
in a cardboard forest
and take me home.

This mule is half horse and half donkey.

Was her horse-mother scared, handled
by an animal so different from her? Three
boys have kissed me in my father's toolshed.

I was scared of all of them.
I was good at shaking. I knocked over
every crusted shovel, every wet rake.

I think the boys were different from me,
though it's hard to tell. I beg

your pardon—tell me again what isn't my body?

What was this field before lighting struck
that one lopsided peach
and burned the grove to the ground?

I don't believe being struck is like an idea
igniting the brain. I don't believe
it feels like (what I think it feels like to) orgasm.

Pleasure never. The word *suddenly*
should not be used. Why do
the men in this town love

the storm? When I race back to the barn
and pull down from the mule's lined back,
it's because I want to be small again. And also

unburned. I'll be happy if nothing chooses me.

Outside our public library
    another magnolia flower withers

        like another delicate, drunk woman
    in a white dress. The loose silk of her forehead

rests on the balcony rail. So it's true.
    There are women outside of bodies.

        Women everywhere. I can't speak
    to every version of a woman, adult and dead,

though they lounge around me, bless
    my iron-soaked bed with swamp stories: saw-

        grass and temper, green animals whose bellies
    fill with the calves of missing women—

you know the ones, they smirk from Florida newspapers, hot
    with ink. This morning one balanced milky ice cubes

        on my lips. What to say back? I broke open
    a blue pack of cigarettes and scribbled down,

I spent a night in the hostel three miles south of where you entered the water.
The beds had been pulled into the garden. For nine dollars a night they'd burn
citronella all around you. [long pause] *When it's that hot, flowers drip oil.*

Perhaps I could've thought of something better
    to tell her if I weren't so clumsy. It is hard. Hard to unhinge

my mouth, especially to a ghost, this one, the most
    gorgeous woman I've ever smelled, her breath

            over the bloated-bottom pitcher, the ice cubes'
        lazy shapes melting into the cream. All I can do is find her

in this dusty newspaper engine. Lord! If there is a church
    for a woman like me it is the second floor of the public library.

        All day I practice women's faces, what I will say.

My Father Takes Me into the Backyard So I Can Become a Woman

He takes a sip of water. He drops a stone into his throat. He takes a sip of water.
The body does not always have to fail,

my father says, forty years from his mother's quick womb. This act is a blessing,
part lesson, that he gives to each daughter when she turns

thirteen. Backyard priest, he kneels in front of the garden hose and rearranges
two smooth stones around a rusted water jug.

I take a sip of water. He drops a stone into my throat. I take a sip of water.
With my father's permission, my hips swell

like the mangrove outside town where boys grow bored and so punch
each other in the mouth over who can hold his breath longest.

Father *yes*. I'm a body of water now. I am stones and I am swamp and I sink
children under the weight of my river, rinse blood from their tongues.

I take a sip of water. He drops a stone into my throat. I take a sip of water.
What am I made of when he says, *Watch how your body endures?*

Notes on How My Mother Gets into Bed

Never forget that we are still animals,
my mother warned me
as she examined the tongue
of my father's young lover.

She pressed it between her thumb
and index finger, her diamond blinding.
My father rubbed his eyes in the ripped-silk
chair. Watched through his fists. For what

was my mother looking?
What could she recognize
in that pink tongue? Beauty,
maybe. I wish she would've told me

to go to my own bed, though I was made
to stand in the doorway. How did the girl
get into our house? New friend?
I wondered if she was sick—

my mother checked her body
like she checked mine
when I was fevered, suffering
from dreams that I was taller

than our barn. We are still animals,
my mother said, fumbling
into bed for days like the most beautiful
warm-blood horse, that careful way—

you can see it—they have to figure out
how to get to the ground. They struggle
with their own body, surrender
the bend, their front knees unlocking

until they kneel, a slow twist of prayer
that it will work and they drop
their back end to the dirt, oh, with that look
like they've hurt themselves, though they had to,

they had to lie down, and then that pant
from their deep-carved nostrils,
which has to be the hottest breath there is
because they squint those weak, wet eyes

for a tender second. Oh my mother, with that
young girl's pulsing tongue between her fingers,
which is nothing a horse could ever do—
oh my mother, *my* mother, she is so tired.

THE YEAR MY FATHER MISTOOK THE OCEAN FOR A MISTRESS

Though I believe everyone has a mother,
I don't know where mine went.

Or which chain-linked street
the veined woman who birthed me
limped off to in her paper hospital gown.

Does she hear my jealous monologue
about the ocean? From the open window
of my father's bedroom, I whine,

I will not write the bright ode the ocean wants;
I have the right to refuse the sea.

On the roof above, my father
adjusts his lavender evening suit
and dreams toward water

with an empty bottle. He climbs
down to the water's edge,
lowers his chin to her foamy hem.

Does he want to swallow and swallow her?
If I could get just one man to take a sip from my elbow.
If I could turn just one man away from the ocean.

I am right to refuse the ocean—
when I climb to the roof
after my father is gone, I lightly choke.

How can I make her gone? I want to wake up
in a country without an ocean at every border.

Her sick rhythm renders me powerless, I tell you, I won't
write the bright poem she wants, she is nothing
like my mother, I don't want any man

to look into the ocean, please don't
look into her, don't, my father, look into her.

The bathroom stall door
swings thin, sings ink,

But I love him.

When the cashier boy sprays
Windex on it, he dreams

that a daddy kissed (just one)
of the young daughters.

How silly. Men kissing
other men's daughters.

The white chairs
in the courtyard
have iron loops

in their backs.
I watch the mothers

that plop on them,
how they drop

birth control pills onto
their daughters' tongues.

(If you take them,
it makes you
want to have sex less.)

How do
the factory men get
the iron to bend?

The Year My Mother and I Mistook the Pool for a Father

If I couldn't sleep I nightgowned out there
and held my breath on top of it.

Who's afraid of the dark? Not me. There should be

something sweet in taking care of your own.
Sweeter than water than blood than honey than tar.

My mother and I mistook our pool
for a clean-shaven man—

she crouched on the edge
and surface-dipped her face. *Left side, right side.*

The night, with its cat-in-a-burlap-sack scent,
made the water look solid.

Like it could kiss back. Why else would it ask
my mother and me to undress?

We decided this was the best way to live.
We set up two chairs and cut our own hair

over the pool. Unhooking
the backs of our dresses, we dove,

floated ovals around each other.
We fountained green

mouthfuls to the deep end, pausing
every now and then like statues

of living women. Of dead women.
The wetness felt honest. (Don't trust

an unwet body.) My mother fed the pool
water fed it blood fed it honey. I said, *Tar?*

No, she said. *He won't be able to handle that.*

Who were we all those nights?
Who were we talking about?

WHITE SKIN

In the illuminated night market, I buy one

        pair of earrings, all mother-
    of-pearl, dripping hard

down my ears. They are the same

        color as my neck!
    So have I been birthed by the ocean

too? Can I be worked into something

        a woman might wear to feel lovely?
    Come on now, Mother, I love you—

Tell me where I came from! You know I fear

        the ocean with its hot swirl—and yet
    you are too beautiful. All calm, all

dark. You never could have made me.

When I say that I'm sleeping
behind my house, I mean

the kitchen lightbulb
swings from a beaded ceiling chain

just beyond my throat. I mean
I can hear the scratch

of our inherited radio
and my mother as she spits

on the cigarette ash in the saucer
because maybe the house will

go up, for once, in flames. I have one
thin white tent, my own bedsheet

taut across two metal folding chairs,
the dried piss and recurring nightmare

just bleached from the fabric,
so when my mother turns

the radio higher, I hear it too:
Nine thousand white refugee tents.

I inch closer to the house.
How do I know that a girl named Phalia

was taken from her mother
with only one dress? I am

across the grass like a breath.
In the radio, the soldier says,

How can I not lift your dress?
And Phalia says, *How*

can you not lift my dress?
I am on my hands and knees.

Does she have to take her clothes off
to wash the dress? That only garment,

that only pair of hands, over and over
and wouldn't it be terrible

if, for once, it ripped up in shreds?
Does a dress have an opening

like a tent? Is it at the throat?
The thighs?

Nine thousand tents, my mother spins
the dial higher until I can't hear

her or the ash or the bulb
on its godless chain. Mother

must be weeping now, her hurt—
it lets out like a breeze. So what

sifts from these thousands
of tents? Women without bedrooms

just upstairs, just inside, I am so close
I can touch the kitchen wall, could

slide fingers in the window. These women
are nothing like me, nothing even

like the woman in the radio.
My mother turns off the program

and I can only think "tent,"
the pole kicked out from underneath,

how it hushes to the ground
like a girl. Phalia. Does she think,

when she's awake, that she's pretty?

I break a thermometer on my bedroom floor.

Hardwood. The mercury in my right palm, I step gently out
to the driveway of my parents' house. Heated

concrete. Heated girl. It is the most shining wet
I have ever seen. But is it killing me?

It isn't hard to imagine the Big Man as a child.
  Over dinner tonight, his jaw worries

    a rib with nothing left. He cracks it open
  and touches the end to his tongue—sweet marrow,

it must be. He closes his eyes. What kind of dinner
  table portrait is this? A bad man in a high-backed chair

    and behind him, the ghosts
  of all the snow-covered animals he's ever eaten.

The wolf he ate wild licks his one killing tooth.
  How did I fall in love?

    The Big Man does not look up
  from the china. *I dare you, darling. Lick me clean.*

A man of tundra, of ice shoe, of frozen lung fears, a man
  who hides in my twin bed and tells me of the mother

    who never let them have heat. Devil temperature.
  Forty-five degrees inside the house. Each night she twisted

the key up the lock to the pantry door. But left the sugar out.
  One glass jar of sugar, belly shaped, offering

    grain so fine it glowed. In darkness,
  her babies crept the stairs with dripping tongues.

The youngest was lifted to the counter
     where she worked the sink knob, got all their hands

          good and wet. One at a time,
     they dipped fingertips into water, into sugar.

Like snow that would not burn them, they licked it off.
     The children returned empty bellied to their iron beds

          for dreams so vivid they blushed in their sleep. This—
this is a mad sweetness. Six little kids learning

what it is to fall in love. And now, the Big Man gnaws fingers.
     If I stay with him, there will be nothing left of me

          but dream. Burnt-trumpet smell. A loosed
     string of pearls and one of them, dissolving inside him like sugar.

*—If a white carnation is placed in a glass of water
with red food coloring, the flower will take the color.*

But this has no womb?

I think of my own ruffled tomb, how it responds with color

like the carnation. If left alone, barely pink. If touched,
russet. *Can I drink this?* All afternoon, schoolgirls dream

and bruise against classroom windows, crossing and un-

crossing their legs, sliding their opal rings off
and switching them to the other hand.

IN THE ABANDONED APARTMENT BEHIND THE
ICE CREAM PARLOR

—after the hurricane, the city without electricity

No light for days—save
    the sick froth released
        from the ice cream parlor. It glows

    in the back alley. It illuminates my bedroom
until I can count my ribs.

Is anyone else ashamed?

How can water make me
    this lonely? I wrestle slumber
        on the floor under a swollen window,

    watching mattresses ruin and bruise
near the sugared gutter. They fill with flood

until their flower patterns confuse themselves—

the orchid in the fabric
    is unrecognizable as a girl
        asking herself questions in the dark.

    If the light is pleasure leaving the cream,
I wish to be that sweetness.

It has no memory. It has no mother

with her whole arm in the purse
    and no child begging for sugar.
        Tonight I am that hungry child, knelt

    over smashed color: light pink and light green and light
yellow. I begin to sour too. I ask it to come back.

I don't care anymore about light, I want pleasure.

The Snake Dancer at the Gentlemen's Club Writes a Letter to Her Younger Self

The lady gardener in the rough gloves asks you for water
because she is dying, about to collapse into your mother's

    red hydrangeas. You get it. Of course you do.
You are seven, which means you are still a hero.

You want so bad to be this woman that you save her
    with the garden hose. Its readied coil. You still believe

    in water. Its easy miracle. A year ago
you would have baptized her, but not today. Instead

    you drench her dark stomach. You know better
than to bother your mother with this small detail—the woman

    you love best in the world suffering heatstroke
in the driveway your father paved the week you were born.

Your mother is a brunette woman, worshiper
of brown. Sienna. Umber. Ochre. Auburn. Russet. And yet

    you came out so opposite.
You crave a woman who mirrors you. In the drugstore

    you study your mother's wet makeup selection, her skin
so many shades and numbers away from your own. May-

belline, your mother smears it on your face Friday evenings
and lets you dance in her church shoes. But who are you?

The lady gardener lies back on the fruit tree, calls her Great Dane
from your backyard where it chases—what? You don't know.

But how cool, this woman who wrangles snakes, translates
their stripes and poisons and the flowers they lie under

and the thorns around the fruit that will kill you.
The lady gardener knows everything. Even now,

as water rinses across her heart, she tells you, *Don't you move;
there's a copperhead behind you.*

Your mother emerges with a check, not yet dry. You think
the ink might be a kind of venom, though you can't prove it.

Not today. Instead you search your pockets
for your Christmas knife. Why you do this, you don't know.

As a young hero it is difficult to decipher
what protects from what harms. You carve

your name into the trunk of that tree, stunned
by how easily the blade carves bark. You are so young.

Know this: When you are nine, the Great Dane
mistakes you for a garden snake. She sinks teeth

into your top lip. Your mother will be inside
applying red eye shadow and settling her stomach

with cream soda. To this day she doesn't hear you scream.
After today the lady gardener cannot visit you.

The dog will be buried five miles from your scar.
Life is tricky, sweet babe. This morning

you revive a woman with hose water. And yet
you cannot tell good from evil, the garden hose from the snake,

the girl you are now from the one who will, one day,
pull that goddamn tree from the garden.

having swallowed—too many purple—mouthfuls—
of the ocean that washes off the Gulf's limp children—I often
shake—so many firsts—that water—one night
big sister brought me out—there—with her high school boys—
woman-shaped bottles of rum under their jackets—
while they watched—I threw it up—golden—
into the dry dunes—and then we went off—
to find the ends of men's unfinished cigars—half—
buried in shadow sand—in the roots of a palm tree—we found
a businessman—sitting swollen with a plastic bag—
over his face—and a face—in black marker—on the bag—
the reporters of the city sat up in their beds—
and I felt like a queen—all that gold in my throat

Song for the Only Other Woman in the Slaughterhouse

—It has been reported that the menstrual cycles
of women in close quarters sync together over time.

Behind the barn, the men say,

> It sounds like
> someone's singing.

Inside the barn, I say,

> It's music, the way I control
> the body part

> that makes me want
> to kiss. I don't have to

> French the double spine
> of the tracks behind
> the slaughterhouse.

> Without rusted lips,
> I can walk home.

Behind the barn, the men say,

> It sounds like
> someone's singing.

Inside the barn, I say,

> It's music,
> the way I can't control
> the body part

> that, without my permission,
> answers women

> with blood. A quarter century
> in this body and still
> it has conversations
> I'm not aware of. I hold

> a water glass to my thigh,
> but get no secrets.

Behind the barn, the men say,

> You must have smelled her,
> the dark-headed woman
> who climbed the ladder

> and gave mosquito fever speeches
> through complicated teeth.

Inside the barn, I say,

> I can't remember
> my mouth opening into black
> curls, sucking so hard

> the air from her neck. Perhaps
> a part of me dragged

a white handkerchief
under her arms while she dreamt

of scraping the gate open
for the fourteen fevered paint horses.

Behind the barn, the men say,

Too brilliant, the body
and its too many bones.
It sounds
like someone's singing.

From inside the barn, I say,
How do I dare live
inside the body

when the dark-headed woman
is the opposite
of the mare on the table?

After that I wanted everything to open.

God forbid someone ask me to set the table, to line
    the knife next to the fork. God

forbid I ride the train next to a man with weak arms.

I don't want to get those images out,
    her breast in my father's open palm, a wet treasure

he'd spent the year searching for—I wanted to peek
    behind his paper mask for that slack mouth, slant smile.

So gently he tilted it into the jar, as if she might

still feel it. I don't want to forget it,
    the way my father washed his hands

and explained the elegance of staples.

Or how the nurses leaned over the flattened half
    and said *how beautiful, how beautiful* it was

and *what a brilliant doctor your father is* and
    tell me again, which daughter are you?

When they wheeled her out of that sterile temple,
    I wanted to follow her. But how

can I say that I don't know her?
    I wanted to cut the cancer out myself.

Stepping down from the grace of the blue drape,
    I could see the little silver barrette

holding the dark wave of her hair and I wondered what
    if I could just open that. What if I could open just like that?

Dream with Right Breast Missing

Setting: The Woods Behind Her Childhood Home.

Young Woman with Desire:
My body feels generous.

Left Breast:
Don't include me in your "generous."
Don't include me in your "cancer."

Shoulders:
I don't need anything, Doctor.
Take. Keep taking.

Red Bird Tired of Singing:
Where do you see a doctor?
These woods are only thick
with the Barefoot Men who kidnap girls.

Young Woman with Desire:
All my dreams end with the dark
wool across their arms
tightening around my waist.

Chorus of Barefoot Men:
I've worked this all out with your parents
and they don't mind.

Young Woman with Desire:
This dream is different.
My right breast is gone.

Collarbone:
Was I asleep for long?

Hundred Mile Creek:
Look at that purple scar.
There must be somethin' can be done.

Young Woman with Desire:
Am I still pretty?

Chorus of Barefoot Men:
We will wait for the next girl
to come out of your parents' house.

Left Knee:
So there won't be chasing in this dream?

Left Breast:
Wait—

Pine Tree:
It will be hard for me to die.

When he pulls up with the rent,
her dress is halfway down
to the pavement.

Her mother screams
from inside the house,
"Collect the scratch—
keep your dress on."

The girl pours a bottle
on her baby's plastic head, lifts
what's left of her dress

to his car engine. Her milk
makes dark the driveway,
the baby doll's lifelike hair.

He says, "When is the next baptism show?"
and leans back on his Buick's hood
with the envelope of hundreds.

"Bless me, girl—the orange groves
in the next neighborhood,
my neighborhood, are on fire.

The ash blows into my apartment
and settles into my work boots,
my chest hair, the pile of ropes,
the bowl of oranges. Ash is the closest

I've come to seeing snow,
though it's nothing
like the danger of your house,

the doorknobs
where your sister's first
tooth dangles from its dental floss string.

You know, I might have to
get out of town for a while.
But I hate to be alone.

I could take you on the road.
I could make you
famous. Young priestess, I promise,

never again will I bother
your father to repaint
my bedroom. I won't admit

I'm locked out. I'll not ask
your mother to pull my hair
from the lion claw bathtub.

Don't you want to not have to be a girl?"
She lets her dress fall to the concrete.
He says, "Kiss your mother good-bye."
He says, "Bless me."

ON SUNDAY NIGHTS THE JUST-BLED GIRL PAINTS THE BIG MAN'S WIFE

It takes seven canvases
to get her fever
right. All night

I stroke out
her hair, the black
in my fingernails long

after I turn the canvases
to the wall. I won't lie;

every Sabbath I dream
of her. I kiss her. I hold her
under water for too long.

My living room crowds
with heated cheekbones.

I can't get these portraits
right. I can't burn them either.
What is it that her fever is

supposed to teach me?
I paint her at a garden party
where she pulls me aside

and wheezes, *You're a nice girl.*
You've got no business
bein' this pretty.

Her temperature runs
one hundred. I can't get her
to admit she'll die

without an ice bath.
Setting down her sweat rag,
she yanks my hair.

Blond, she says. *No wonder*
he went after you.

Her bangs are soaked
every time I paint them.
What bad news does she try

to rinse from her brain?
My lover, would I be better
if I practiced lying

under water? Go get
your gold stopwatch,

the one she gave you
for your last anniversary. Time
your good little girl.

Pull back the shower curtain.
See how long I can stand it.

she offers her mind—tired—as the orphanage's washing machine—
what dull sheets—collect—and wet in her knobbed skull—

as she considers her three-hours father
in the orphanage office she bleeds—onto his hands to prove her age—

and he—adjusting his wet lenses—yelps into the paperwork—"I'll take her"—
there is the word *all* and there is the word *nothing*—

and in the orange grove—between them—the man lights up—
the cigar he's kept in his underwear drawer—for a year—

because she is on her back—the ash is moon colored—
when he taps it into her collarbone—and she raises—a tiny fist—

she's not allowed back into his car—though he leaves her—
close enough—to the orphanage so she can stumble there—

as he drives back—to his real family—the laughter—
of his bruises—so fresh—he rolls the windows down

REVISING WHAT IS MINE

The university boys, released from their anatomy

courses, empty their rented houses
and return to their mothers' summer blouses. Mine tells me,

Baby, let's get it all out to the edge of the lawn—

The shredded peach love seat and the carved argument table.
The bookshelves are now useless. And the dressers.

Drawer by drawer, university boys pull apart their dressers.

It's lighter this way, baby

Out of every door, boys waltz the big wooden bodies
of their dressers. They can't be bothered with selling,

Just get it all out, all of it, out

and their mother's areolas call them back faded.

University boys cover lawns with dressers
and the dressers break my heart like no boy can.

Are you not coming with me?

Four hours north and he's back in his mother. I haven't left
the front step. There's an *already over you* static from the power lines.

Mine is a quiet paradise—all drenched sour

The man with eight fingers *invaded* me
at the Christmas party where nervous champagne cocktails were served.
Scientist, these are not similar events.

*

The Scientist says the tunneled blossoms from those trees can ruin
the paint on a car. But we love beautiful. Must love beautiful.

We will still let the flowers fall onto the teenagers' lined-up
Fords. They barely thud! They just rub gently, seize

the engine until the teenagers, oily-kissing inside, can't drive.

*

When I can't sleep and there are no helpful siblings
down the hallway struggling to breathe through revisions
of Christmas lists and envelope glue tongue,

I reach back to my childhood and imagine these trees
as faded cartoons. They hover over the wet edge of the lake
with their branchy arms waving, toothless mouths gaping.

They can bend their heads to the ground,
but they can't move their feet.

Aren't we like that?
Most of the time, aren't we just like that?

What I Remember of Standing Outside His House

Only the swamp town's great refusal of dryness—

men with no thirst and children with no thirst and women
filling glasses on the edges of warped porches with only water

and soap. As though I should be baptized a second time. I was
a girl bound by her only dress and the street said

only one thing to me. Sweet Jesus, how everyone came running.

The Just-Bled Girl Wipes Red Juice from Her Lower Lip

It stains her hands, but still
    she rids the bowl of its berries

        and runs them to the backyard,
    bleeding into her nightgown.

Because she believes soil might prove
    the best healer, she returns

        red skin to the ground. Unburst,
    the Big Man discovers her night burial

from two houses away. She paws earth
    on hands and knees when he interrupts

        her dig rhythm, says, *You'd be
easier to love if you were well fed.*

How does the berries' young blood not spill
    before they arrive at his bowl?

        At his jaw? Her flesh rashes paisley
    wallpaper when he comes near.

If she can save one thing. Let these
    bruised skins not rupture. Sugared,

she turns to him and answers, *Watch me.*
Watch my throat open like a sink, watch

my ripening, my tightening. The moonlight, she slices it
with a fist that lifts to her chin. *Watch me*

suckle red drips from my middle finger.

I never thought the oleander like me—

but riding my bicycle by the tree—I throw it—from under
like a lover—I have to examine—this pink-flower shrub—it writhes
outside the nighttime soda factory—it's what I look like

when the Big Man touches—so I want to do things to it—
I want to lift its Christmas dress—I want to make it promise—not to tell—
I want it to stare in the hallway mirror and blame itself for years—

I want it to knock my hand away—I want—to cover the oleander's mouth—
but I can't find it—I—never—thought the oleander like me—but tonight—
I want to push it in a closet—I want—its mind to drift somewhere else—

aren't I supposed to do back—am I remembering the rule right—
golden—I wrap my legs around it until it starts to—milk—and bend—

where are its parents in all this hot wind?

THE JUST-BLED GIRL WRITES A PETITION ON HOTEL PAPER

—for Tallahassee, Florida

Like a child, I hide in the hotel bathtub and fall asleep
with dreams of Lieutenant Bradford's pine box coffin.

How I am in there. I make love to him
as kudzu grows fresh from his mouth.

I love you, Tallahassee, but be a mother to me—knife
the umbilical cord, send me north

to a strawberry field. Let my feet be covered
with anything that looks like hearts. I don't want

to hear the strand of leftover Christmas bells
on the diner door as the husbands shuffle in and beg

waitresses to take them home
and cough quarters onto their stomachs. I love you,

Tallahassee, but too many pool-flavored infants are forgotten
in your thrift store rocking chairs. They wake hours later

on the shelf of broken toasters and so I beg you,
Tallahassee, I love you, let me leave.

Too often I hunt your backstreets, those graveyards
of sunburned cash registers. I finger the drawers

until the rosary beads wither in my jeans. Tallahassee,
the unhemmed skirt girls so much as see me

and they lock themselves in the gas station bathroom.
Is it you who presses their chapped lips to the mirror?

I love you, Tallahassee; it has been a beautiful time here,
thank you so much for your floorboard religion, the hymns

coupled with bottles of bleach, and the wives
scrubbing Bible ink from their pubic hair. I love you;

thank you so much for having me, you generous city
with your sweet sons who keep their sheets clean

and that Big Man, fifty, who has just slipped another hotel key
under the rusted dumpster. Tallahassee, if we never

see each other again, know that I am grateful for the maid
who blots blood from the carpet with stationery.

JOHN ASHBERY
Selected Poems
Self-Portrait in a Convex Mirror

TED BERRIGAN
The Sonnets

LAUREN BERRY
The Lifting Dress

JOE BONOMO
Installations

PHILIP BOOTH
Selves

JIM CARROLL
*Fear of Dreaming: The Selected
    Poems*
Living at the Movies
Void of Course

ALISON HAWTHORNE DEMING
Genius Loci
Rope

CARL DENNIS
Callings
*New and Selected Poems
    1974-2004*
Practical Gods
Ranking the Wishes
Unknown Friends

DIANE DI PRIMA
Loba

STUART DISCHELL
Backwards Days
Dig Safe

STEPHEN DOBYNS
*Velocities: New and Selected
    Poems, 1966–1992*

EDWARD DORN
*Way More West: New and
    Selected Poems*

ADAM FOULDS
The Broken Word

CARRIE FOUNTAIN
Burn Lake

AMY GERSTLER
Crown of Weeds: Poems
Dearest Creature
Ghost Girl
Medicine
Nerve Storm

EUGENE GLORIA
Drivers at the Short-Time Motel
Hoodlum Birds

DEBORA GREGER
*Desert Fathers, Uranium
    Daughters*
God
Men, Women, and Ghosts
Western Art

TERRANCE HAYES
Hip Logic
Lighthead
Wind in a Box

ROBERT HUNTER
Sentinel and Other Poems

MARY KARR
Viper Rum

WILLIAM KECKLER
Sanskrit of the Body

JACK KEROUAC
Book of Sketches
Book of Blues
Book of Haikus

JOANNA KLINK
Circadian
Raptus

JOANNE KYGER
As Ever: Selected Poems

ANN LAUTERBACH
Hum
*If In Time: Selected Poems,
    1975–2000*
On a Stair
Or to Begin Again

CORINNE LEE
PYX

PHILLIS LEVIN
May Day
Mercury

WILLIAM LOGAN
Macbeth in Venice
Strange Flesh
The Whispering Gallery

ADRIAN MATEJKA
Mixology

MICHAEL MCCLURE
*Huge Dreams: San Francisco and
    Beat Poems*

DAVID MELTZER
*David's Copy: The Selected Poems
    of David Meltzer*

CAROL MUSKE-DUKES
An Octave above Thunder

Red Trousseau
Twin Cities

ALICE NOTLEY
Culture of One
The Descent of Alette
Disobedience
In the Pines
Mysteries of Small Houses

LAWRENCE RAAB
The History of Forgetting
*Visible Signs: New and
    Selected Poems*

BARBARA RAS
The Last Skin
One Hidden Stuff

PATTIANN ROGERS
Generations
Wayfare

WILLIAM STOBB
Nervous Systems

TRYFON TOLIDES
An Almost Pure Empty Walking

ANNE WALDMAN
Kill or Cure
Manatee/Humanity
*Structure of the World Compared
    to a Bubble*

JAMES WELCH
Riding the Earthboy 40

PHILIP WHALEN
Overtime: Selected Poems

ROBERT WRIGLEY
Beautiful Country
*Earthly Meditations: New and
    Selected Poems*
Lives of the Animals
Reign of Snakes

MARK YAKICH
*The Importance of Peeling
    Potatoes in Ukraine*
*Unrelated Individuals Forming a
    Group Waiting to Cross*

JOHN YAU
Borrowed Love Poems
Paradiso Diaspora